NATIONAL
GEOGRAPHIC

✓ W9-BNA-624

The Sun

PIONEER EDITION

By Fran Downey

CONTENTS

The

By Fran Downey

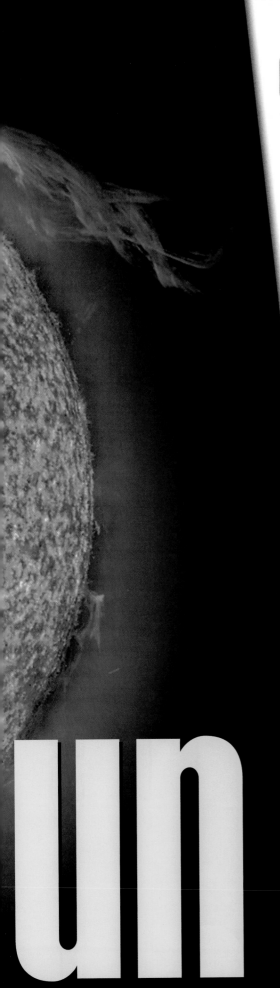

Our sun may look like a small yellow ball in the sky. But things are not always as they seem. For one, the sun is big. A million Earths could fit inside it!

A Real Star

The sun is a **star.** It is a huge ball of glowing gases. Like other stars, our sun is full of energy. It gives off a lot of light and heat.

Our sun warms Earth and other planets too. Without it, life on Earth would be impossible.

Star Studies

The sun looks different than other stars. That's because the sun is much closer to Earth.

The sun is just 93 million miles away. That might not sound very close. Yet in space, it is just around the corner.

Some stars are a few trillion miles from Earth. Most stars are much farther away.

Star Power. *The sun is a stormy star. It is made of hot gases that bubble on its surface.*

Color Coded

From Earth, most stars look like tiny white dots. Yet stars come in different colors. Their colors tell us how hot they are.

Blue stars are the hottest. Their surface can be a sizzling 20,000°F.
Yellow stars are medium hot. Their surface is about 10,000°F.
Red stars are cool. Their surface is only about 5,000°F.

Our Yellow Star

What kind of star is our sun? It is a yellow star. So it is not too hot or cool. It is just right for life on Earth.

The sun's surface is not all yellow. Pictures of the sun show dark areas called **sunspots.** Sunspots are much cooler than the rest of the surface. So they look dark.

Scientists have studied sunspots for many years. We know sunspots come and go. Sometimes the sun has only a few. Over time, more appear. Then they go away. We don't know why.

In the Loop. *You could stack ten Earths beneath these arches of superhot gas.*

Changes on the Sun

The sun is always changing. Its surface bubbles with hot gases.

Sometimes gases around the sun cause explosions. Huge arches of hot gas loop up from the sun. Then they fall back to the surface.

Other times the sun sends out giant **flares.** These are streams of light and heat. They race away from the sun.

Spots of Trouble? *This picture shows big sunspots on the sun's surface. Just a few days later, a huge solar flare erupted. It was the largest ever recorded.*

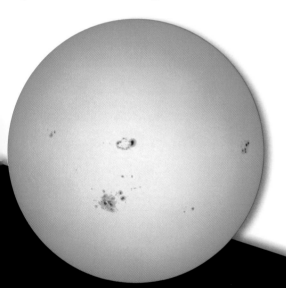

Problems With Flares

Flares blast into space. They can stretch thousands of miles away from the sun. Some even come close to Earth.

Flares can harm our **satellites.** These are machines that travel around Earth. We depend on satellites. Some help us study weather. Others send radio or TV signals.

Luckily, scientists are learning more about flares. Someday they might be able to predict flares. That would help protect satellites.

This is just one reason to study the sun. Our sun can also help us understand life on Earth. It can teach us about other stars too.

 What are some of the ways that our sun affects Earth?

Wordwise

flare: stream of energy that comes from the sun

star: ball of gas in space that can make heat and light

sunspot: dark, cooler area on the sun's surface

satellite: object that circles a planet, such as a machine that circles Earth

1 Flare

Magnetic Field 2

3 Core

Inside the Sun

4 Sunspots

5 Photosphere

6 Chromosphere

7 Corona

1 Flare: giant explosion that makes a powerful stream of energy

2 Magnetic Field: invisible electric currents that act like huge magnets (The large loops seen on the surface are part of the field.)

3 Core: huge furnace in center of the sun that makes heat and light

4 Sunspots: dark areas that are cooler than the rest of the sun's surface

5 Photosphere: visible surface that we see from Earth

6 Chromosphere: inner layer of the sun's atmosphere

7 Corona: outer layer of the sun's atmosphere

Earth

AND THE Sun

You may not think about the sun much. It rises and it sets—end of story. Well, think again. Energy from the sun makes life on Earth possible.

Heating Up Earth

Without the sun, Earth would be a different place. There would be no plants or animals. There would be no people. Our planet would be a frozen rock in space.

Thankfully, we have the sun. It warms Earth. You can feel the sun's heat on a hot summer day.

The sun warms our planet in winter too. A winter day may feel cold. But the sun is always giving off heat and warming Earth.

Food From the Sun

The sun does not just warm our planet. It also gives us light. Plants and animals need sunlight to live.

Plants use sunlight to make their own food. They store the energy from sunlight. Plants use this energy to live and grow.

Animals are not like plants. They cannot make their own food. Many get energy from eating plants. This energy came from the sun. It started out as sunlight!

Food Energy. *Plants, such as this corn, use energy from the sun to grow. In turn, plants give animals energy to live.*

VIRGINIA GROSSMAN/SHUTTERSTOCK

Colors of the Rainbow

Sunlight also brings color to our world. That is because sunlight is really made of colors. Don't believe it? Just look at a rainbow.

A rainbow forms when sunlight hits rain. The sunlight travels inside raindrops. It bends. Then a band of colors appears in the sky.

You see red, orange, yellow, green, blue, indigo, and violet. These are the colors of a rainbow. They are also the colors in light.

Sun Power

The sun gives us colors, food, and warmth. But that is not all. We also use the sun as a source of power.

Solar cells change sunlight into electricity. Small solar cells can run toys. Big solar cells can power cars and homes. They can even run satellites in space!

The sun affects our lives in many ways. It is a powerful source of energy. The sun makes life on our planet possible.

Colors in the Sky.
A rainbow shows the many colors that make up sunlight.

The Sun

Answer these questions to find out what you learned about this hot topic.

1 Why does the sun look different to us than other stars?

2 What is the difference between blue, yellow, and red stars?

3 What kind of star is our sun?

4 What are flares? How can they cause problems for people?

5 How is the sun important to life on Earth?

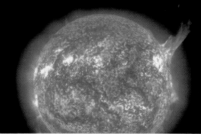